B-I-N-G-O!

ISBN 0-439-68360-2

16 15 14 12 13 14/0

Printed in the U.S.A. 40
First printing, September 2004

Book design by Jennifer Rinaldi

B-I-N-G-O!

Illustrated by
Hans Wilhelm

READ WITH ME
Cartwheel
·B·O·O·K·S·®
PAPERBACKS

SCHOLASTIC INC.
New York Toronto London Auckland Sydney
Mexico City New Delhi Hong Kong Buenos Aires

There was a farmer had a dog,

And Bingo was
his name-o!

BINGO
ZZZ

B-I-N-G-O!

B-I-N-G-O!

B-I-N-G-O!

And Bingo was his name-o!

There was a farmer had a dog,

And Bingo was his name-o!

ZZZ

And Bingo was his name-o!

There was a farmer had a dog,

And Bingo was his name-o!

ZZZ

And Bingo was his name-o!

There was a farmer had a dog,
And Bingo was his name-o!

ZZZ

Clap! Clap! Clap!
– – – G – O!
Clap! Clap! Clap!
– – – G – O!
Clap! Clap! Clap!
– – – G – O!
And Bingo was his name-o!

There was a farmer had a dog,

And Bingo was his name-o!

ZZZ

Clap!
Clap!
Clap!
Clap!
-
-
-
-O!
Clap!
Clap!
Clap!
Clap!
-
-
-
-O!
Clap!
Clap!
Clap!
Clap!
-
-
-
-O!
And Bingo was his name-o!

There was a farmer had a dog,
And Bingo was his name-o!

Clap!
Clap!
Clap!
Clap!
Clap!
Clap!
Clap!
Clap!
Clap!
Clap!
Clap!
Clap!

Clap!
lap!
lap!

And

BINGO
was his name-o!

B-I-N-G-O!

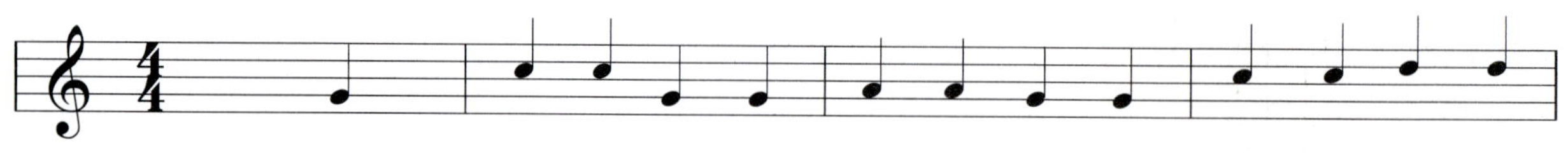

There was a farm - er had a dog, and Bin - go was his

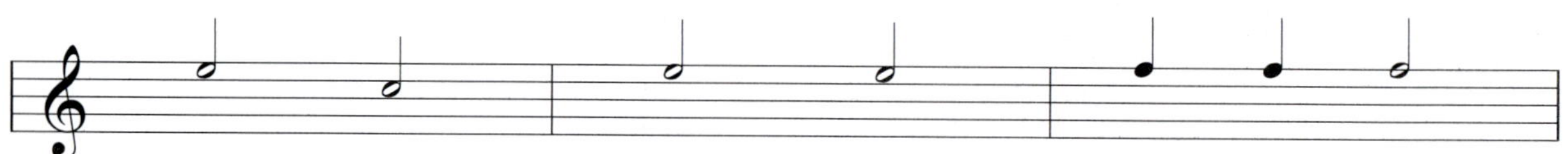

name - o, B - I - N - G - O,

B - I - N - G - O, B - I

N - G - O, and Bin - go was his name - o!